15 RECITAL SONGS IN ENGLISH

Songs by
ARGENTO, ... FINZI,
HEAD, IR... OREM
and VAUGHAN WILLIAMS

To access companion recorded diction lessons and piano accompaniments online, visit:

www.halleonard.com/mylibrary

Enter Code
2573-5101-0002-0058

BOOSEY & HAWKES

DISTRIBUTED BY

Hal•LEONARD®

7777 W. BLUEMOUND RD. P.O. BOX 13819 MILWAUKEE, WI 53213

www.boosey.com
www.halleonard.com

CONTENTS

Pianist on the recordings: Laura Ward

for Nicholas Di Virgilio
Dirge
from *Six Elizabethan Songs*
original key

WILLIAM SHAKESPEARE

DOMINICK ARGENTO

poco più mosso

My shroud of white stuck all with yew, O pre - pare it!___ O pre-

pare it!___ My part of death, no one so true Did__ share it.___

Did__ share it._____ **Tempo I** Not a flower,

not a flower sweet On my black cof - fin let there be strown;_____

To Beata Mayer
The Ash Grove
Welsh Tune
from *Folksong Arrangements Volume 1: British Isles*
original key

Arranged by
BENJAMIN BRITTEN

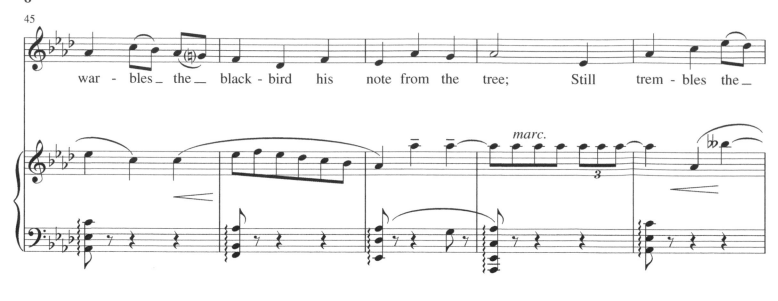

war - bles _ the _ black-bird his note from the tree; Still trem - bles the _

moon-beam on stream - let _ and _ foun - tain, But what are _ the _ beau - ties of

na - ture to me. With sor - row, _ deep _ sor - row, my bos - om _ is _

lad - en All day I go mourn - ing in search of my love. Ye

express.

ech - oes, O tell me, where is the sweet maid - en? She sleeps 'neath the

green turf down by the Ash - grove.

O Waly, Waly

from Somerset (Cecil Sharp) *
from *Folksong Arrangements Volume 3: British Isles*
original key

Arranged by
BENJAMIN BRITTEN

O, love is hand - some and love is fine, and love's a

jew - el while it is new, But when it is old, it grow - eth _

cold, and fades a - way like morn - ing _ dew.

To Clytie Mundy

The Salley Gardens

Irish Tune

from *Folksong Arrangements Volume 1: British Isles*

original key

Arranged by
BENJAMIN BRITTEN

*W. B. YEATS

*The words of this song are reprinted from "Collected Poems of W. B. Yeats" by permission of Mrs. Yeats.

shoul - der she _ laid her _ snow - white hand; She bid me _ take life eas - y as the grass grows _ on _ the _ weirs, But _ I was _ young and _ fool - ish, and _ now am _ full of tears.

Simple Gifts

Shaker Song

from *Old American Songs, First Set*

original key: A♭ Major

Arranged by
AARON COPLAND

[2nd time to Coda]

love and de - light. _____ When true sim - pli - ci - ty is gained To

mf (plainly)

Ped.

bow and to bend we shan't be a-shamed To turn, turn will be our de-light 'Till by

Ped.

turn- ing, turn-ing we come round right. _____ 'Tis the

CODA

(dreamily)

rit.

At the River

Hymn Tune
from *Old American Songs, Second Set*
original key: E♭ Major

Arranged by
AARON COPLAND

Soon our hap - py hearts will quiv - er With the mel - o - dy of ___

peace. Yes we'll gath - er by the riv - er, The

beau - ti - ful, the beau - ti - ful ___ riv - er, Gath - er with the saints ___ by the

riv - er That flows by the throne of ___ God, ___ That flows by the throne of ___ God.

Fear no more the heat o' the sun

from *Let Us Garlands Bring*

original key: B♭ Major

WILLIAM SHAKESPEARE

GERALD FINZI

wag- es: Gold - en lads and girls all must, As chim - ney-sweep-ers,

come to dust.

Fear no more the frown o' the great; Thou art past the ty-rant's stroke:

Care no more to clothe and eat; To thee the reed

is as the oak: The scep - tre, learn - ing, phys - ic, must All fol-low this, and come to dust. Fear no more the light - ning-flash, Nor the all-dread-ed thun - der - stone; Fear not slan - der, cen - sure rash;

Thou hast fin - ished joy and moan: All lov - ers

young, all lov - ers must Con - sign to thee, and

come to dust.

p crescendo poco a poco

No ex - or - cis - er harm thee! Nor no witch - craft

charm thee! Ghost un - laid for - bear thee! Noth-ing ill come

near thee! Qui - et con - sum - ma - tion have;

And re - nown - èd be _____ thy grave! _____

Oh fair to see

from *Oh fair to see*

original key

CHRISTINA ROSSETTI

GERALD FINZI

Oh fair to see

Bloom - la - den cher - ry tree, Ar - rayed in sun - ny white, An

A - pril day's de - light; Oh fair to see!

To Hester Berry

Money, O!

from *Songs of the Countryside*

original key: G minor

W.H. DAVIES

MICHAEL HEAD

18 *mp*

how their wives do hum like bees A - bout their work from morn till night.____

poco rit. *mf*

So, when I hear these poor ones

23 *f a tempo*

laugh,_____ And see the rich ones cold - ly frown—

25 *ten.* *mf* *poco rit.*

Poor men, think I, need not go up So much as rich men__ should come

Headley Down, Sept. 1928

Spring Sorrow

original key: F Major

RUPERT BROOKE

JOHN IRELAND

This Poem is reprinted from "1914 and other Poems" by Rupert Brooke,
by permission of the Literary Executor and Messrs Sidgwick and Jackson Ltd.

pain. My __ heart all Win - ter lay so numb, The

earth so dead and frore, That I nev - er thought __ the

Spring would come, Or my heart wake an - y more. But

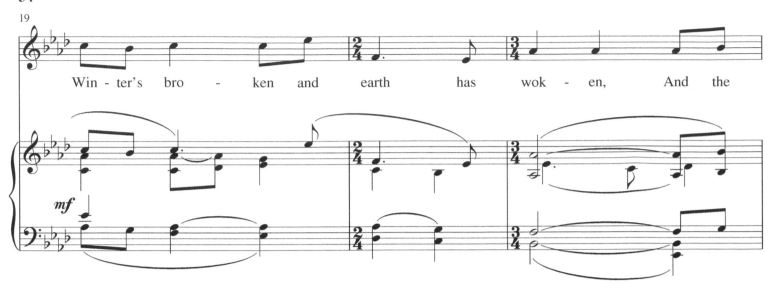

Win - ter's bro - ken and earth has wok - en, And the

small birds cry a - gain; And the haw - thorn hedge __ puts forth its buds And my

heart puts forth its pain. _____

April, 1918

To the memory of Arnold Guy Vivian

Drink to me only with thine eyes

BEN JONSON

from *Arnold Book of Old Songs*

original key: E♭ Major

English Melody
18th Century
Arranged by
ROGER QUILTER

ask a drink___ di - vine;_____ But might I of Jove's

nec - tar sup,___ I would___ not change for thine.

I sent thee late a

ro - sy wreath,___ Not so___ much honour - ing thee,_____

To the memory of my friend, Mrs. Cary-Elwes

Weep you no more

from *Seven Elizabethan Lyrics*

original key

ANONYMOUS

ROGER QUILTER

Weep you no more, sad foun - tains; What

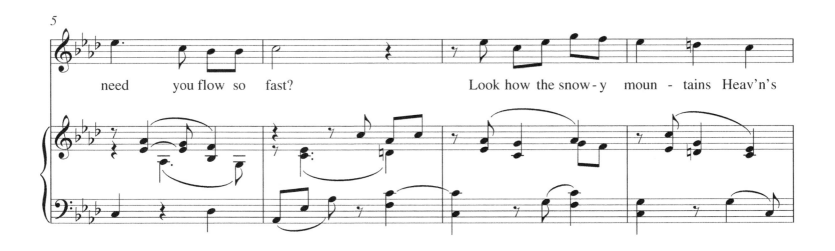

need you flow so fast? Look how the snow - y moun - tains Heav'n's

sun doth gent - ly waste! But my Sun's heav'n-ly eyes View not your

To Shirley Xenia Gabis Rhoads

Love
original key

THOMAS LODGE

NED ROREM

pain,   Love meets me   in   the   shade a - gain;   Want I to

walk   in   se - cret   grove,   E'en there I   meet   with   sa - cred

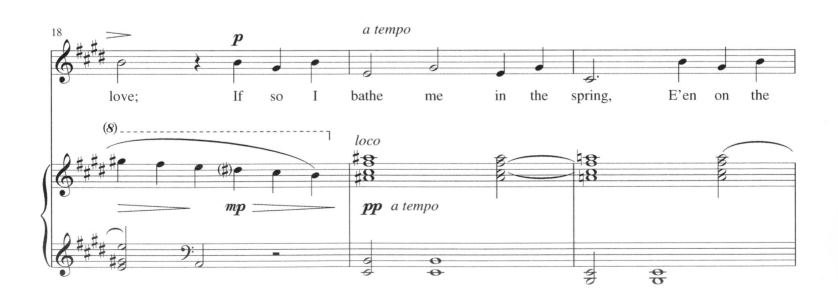

love;   If so   I   bathe   me   in   the   spring,   E'en on the

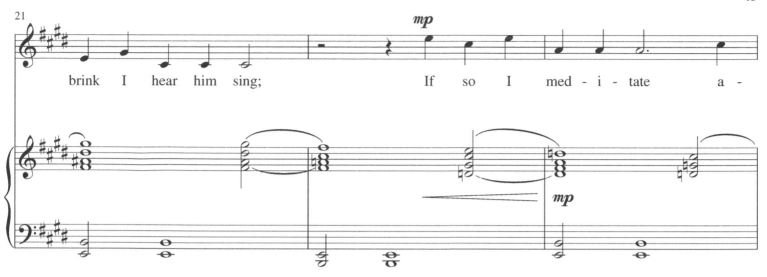

Hyères, 22 July 1953

To Nell Tangeman

Little Elegy
original key

ELINOR WYLIE

NED ROREM

Andante (♩ = 66)

With - out you No _ rose can grow; _ No _ leaf _ be _ green _ If _ nev - er seen _ Your _ sweet - est face; _ No _ bird have grace _ Or _ power to sing; _ Or _ an - y - thing _ Be _ kind, _ or fair, _ And _ you no - where. _

p dolce, senza espressione

mp   *p*

p espr.   *dim.*   *e*   *rit.*   *pp*

ppp

New York City, 28 March 1948
(Spring, cool, bright, noon)

Bright is the ring of words

from *Songs of Travel*

original key: D Major

ROBERT LOUIS STEVENSON

RALPH VAUGHAN WILLIAMS

Bright is the ring of words ____ When the right man rings them, Fair the fall of songs ____ when the sing - er sings them. Still they are car - olled and said – On